Annic Hurtrer

Let's Scoubidou

Search Press

Measurement chart		
Metric		**Imperial**
1 millimetre [mm]		0.03937 in
1 centimetre [cm]	10 mm	0.3937 in
5 centimetres	50 mm	2 in
10 centimetres	100 mm	4 in
50 centimetres	500 mm	20 in
1 metre [m]	100 cm	40 in

For Jean-Claude Painsecq

First published in Great Britain 2005

Search Press Limited
Wellwood, North Farm Road
Tunbridge Wells, Kent TN2 3DR

Originally published in France by Le Temps Apprivoisé
7, rue des Canettes, 75006 Paris
© 2004, LTA, a department of Meta-Éditions
Original title: Scoubidous Vol. 2

English translation by Linda Black
for First Edition Translations Ltd, Cambridge, England

English translation © Search Press Ltd, 2005

ISBN 1 84448 142 5

Photographs: Charlie Abad

Graphic Design: Thomas Bayle

Manufactured by Chromographique

Printed in Spain by A. G. Elkar S. Coop, 48180 Loiu (Bizkaia)

Introduction

You are going to discover or rediscover the atmosphere of the sixties by weaving together multicoloured strands. Seventy new ideas combine scoubidous with polystyrene balls and coloured foam…
to create original objects.

Contents

Tools and materials

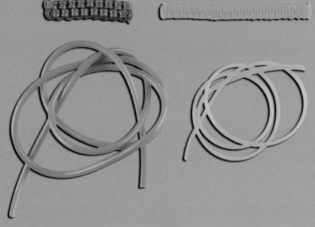

Plastic strands

The scoubidou strands sold in shops measure between 0.90 m and 1 m. There are different colours and thicknesses. According to the thickness of the strand used, you will obtain a thicker or thinner scoubidou.

Scissors

Use embroidery scissors. As they are small and pointed, they will cut the plastic strands accurately.

Pieces of wire

The wire helps "arm" the scoubidou. When slid into the scoubidou strand or stitch, it makes it rigid and maintains the shapes you wish to obtain.

Wire cutters

These are essential for cutting the wire used to arm the scoubidous.

Soldering iron

This is used to fuse the end of the scoubidou. If you preheat the tip of a screwdriver, it will have the same effect.

Craft knife

This is for cutting the foam sheets and scoubidous. It is advisable to lay them on top of some cardboard or on a cutting board before cutting.

Glue

This is used to stick the foam onto the scoubidous and for sticking the scoubidous together.

Foam sheets

2 mm thick and in various colours, foam sheets are used to create shapes.

Starting off a scoubidou

There are 2 ways of starting off a scoubidou.

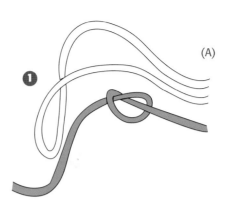

You will need

2 plastic strands or
4 plastic strands

First method

1 Take 2 strands, make a knot in the centre of the first strand (A), then a loop in the middle of the second strand, and tie them together (B).

2 When you assemble the 2 strands, you can slide on a ring or an object.

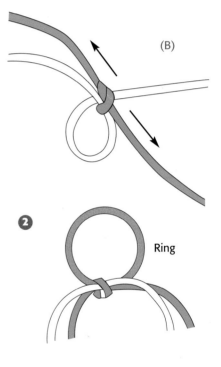

Second method

Take 4 strands and tie them together at one end.

However many strands you use to make a scoubidou, you always start it off the same way. By tying a knot at one end, you can produce a scoubidou that is twice as long as with the loop technique. For beginners, the loop allows you to hold the scoubidou whilst you are making it.

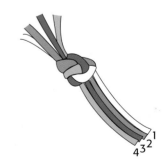

Simple scoubidou

Square stitch

If you start off with 2 strands of different colours, the scoubidou is bicoloured. When tying together 4 strands at one end, use 1, 2, 3 or 4 strand colours. However you start off, the square-stitch technique is identical. The drawings opposite illustrate the square stitch starting with a loop.

You will need

2 or 4 plastic strands

To make it

① Flip strand 1 over strand 3.

② Flip strand 2 over strand 4.

③ Flip strand 4 over strand 2 and through strand 1.

④ Flip strand 3 over strand 1 and through strand 2.

⑤ Pull the 4 strands tight. You will obtain a square-shaped stitch.

Start again from step 1 up to step 5. You will then obtain a second row. Then continue with steps 1 to 5 until you obtain the length you want.

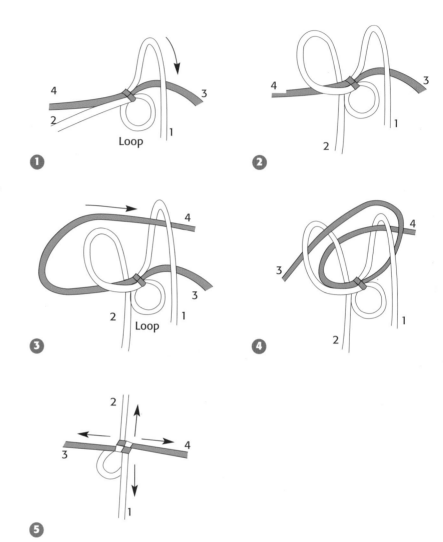

Round (turning) stitch

Just like the square stitch, use either of the two starting-off methods. The main difference between the square stitch and the turning stitch lies in step 1.

You will need

2 or 4 plastic strands

To make it

1 Flip strand 3 over strand 2 and between strands 2 and 4.

2 Flip strand 4 over strand 1.

3 Thread strand 2 through strand 4.

4 Flip strand 1 over strand 4 and thread it through the loop formed by strand 3.

5 Pull the 4 strands tight.

Start again from step 1 and go up to step 5. You will obtain the second row that turns as it grows. Continue with steps 1 to 5 until you obtain the size you want.

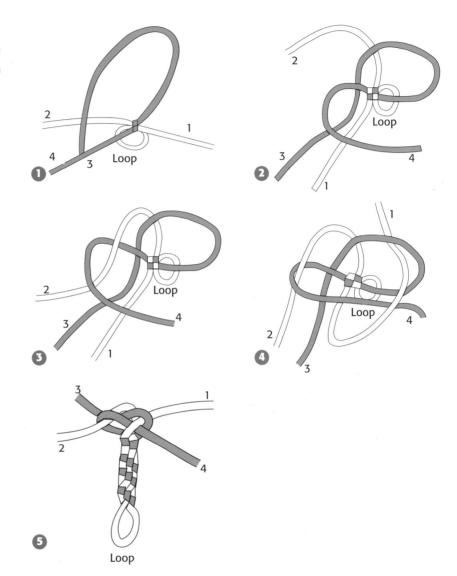

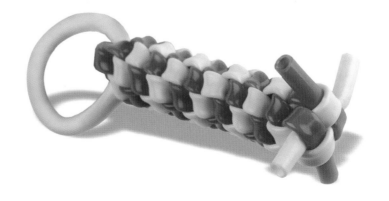

Scoubidous

Rectangular scoubidou

You will need

6 plastic strands

To make it

1. Tie together 6 strands at one end or make a loop with 3 strands.

2. Gather together strands 5 and 6 next to strand 1, then flip strand 4 over strand 2, and strand 3 over strand 1 in the opposite direction (this step is identical to steps 1 and 2 for the square-stitch simple scoubidou).

3. Make the same loops with strands 5 and 6, flip strand 5 over strand 1 and strand 6 over strand 2, each in one direction.

4. Take strand 1, thread it through the loop formed by strand 5 and the loop formed by strand 3.

5. Thread strand 2 through the loop formed by strand 4, then through the loop formed by strand 6.

6. Pull the 6 strands tight. You will obtain a rectangular shape made up of 2 squares. Start again from step 1 and go up to step 5 to obtain a second row and so on and so forth until you have obtained the size you want. (Strands 1 and 2 decrease twice as fast as the other strands.)

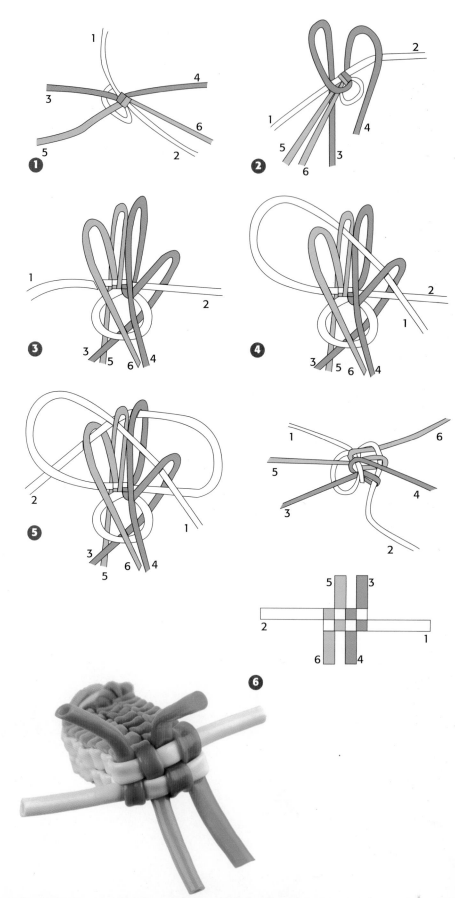

8

Spiral stitch scoubidou

You will need

6 plastic strands

To make it

1. Tie together 6 strands at one end or make a loop by tying together 3 strands in the same way as for rectangular scoubidous.

2. The first turn of this scoubidou is identical to that used for the rectangular one.

3. After the last turn – that is to say, steps 1 and 2 – the position of the strands is different.

4. Steps 3 and 4 consist of weaving strands 1 and 2 in the same way as for the rectangular stitch.

Pull the 6 strands tight. Start again from step 1 up to the tightening to obtain a second row and so on and so forth, until you have obtained the size you want.

Just as with the rectangular scoubidou technique, the length of the 2 strands that cross the other 4 is going to decrease twice as fast.

You can combine both techniques by creating 5 rows of rectangular stitching and then 6 rows of spiral stitching.

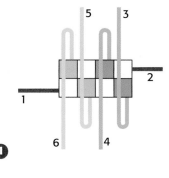

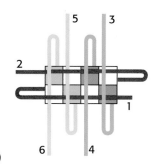

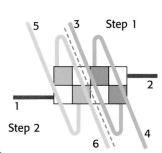

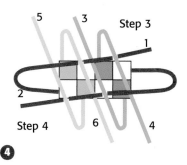

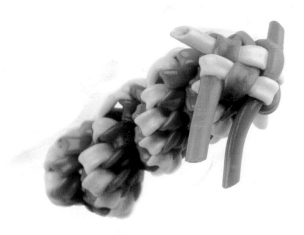

9

Double scoubidou

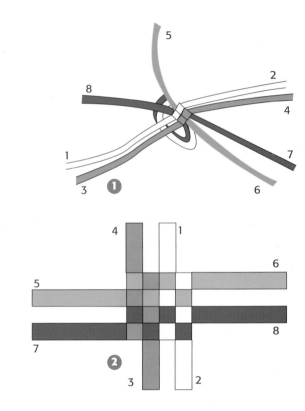

You will need

8 plastic strands

To make it

1 Tie together 8 strands at one end or make a double loop by tying it to the knots of the other 2 strands.

The technique is identical to that for 6 strands (page 9).

Make 4 loops using steps 1 and 2 and start again.

Repeat steps 3 and 4 twice to thread your extra strand.

2 Once tightened, you will obtain a square made up of 4 squares.

For the round-shaped scoubidou, follow the technique for 6 spiral strands by repeating steps 3 and 4 after tightening. You will obtain a square that will turn as you progress with your creation.

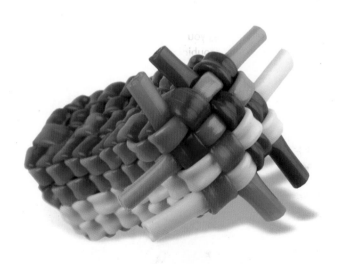

Hexagonal stitch scoubidou

You will need

6 plastic strands

To make it

1. Tie together 6 strands at one end.

2. Make a loop with strand number 2, place it inside number 1, flip number 1 over number 2 and place it inside number 6, flip number 6 over number 1 and place it inside number 4, flip number 4 over number 5 and place it inside number 3, flip number 3 over number 4, and place it inside the loop made at the start with strand number 2.

3. Pull tight by holding 3 strands (1, 2, 3) in one hand and the other 3 (4, 5, 6) in the other hand. Repeat the operation by holding strands 2, 3 and 4 in one hand and strands 5, 6 and 1 in the other. Continue to pull tight in this way by changing strands with each turn, until the strands are arranged evenly.

Variation A
By repeating the weaving, you will obtain a round-shaped scoubidou.

Variation B
By repeating the weaving, you will obtain a hexagonal-shaped scoubidou.

With 5 strands, you will obtain a pentagonal scoubidou; with 7 strands, a heptagonal scoubidou; and with 8 strands, an octagonal scoubidou.

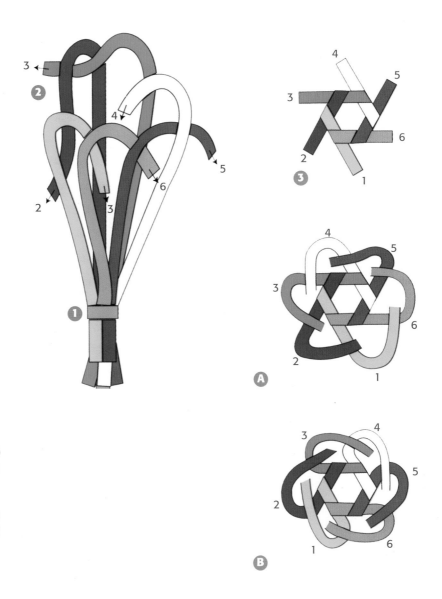

11

Arming the scoubidou

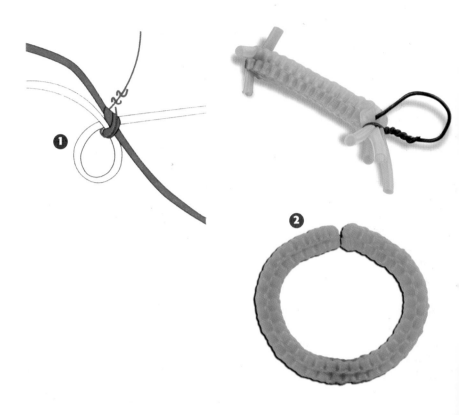

You will need

Wire
Wire cutters

To make it

To make a scoubidou rigid and retain the twists, you have to arm the scoubidou.

1. From the start, fix some wire to the first loop and place the strands on either side of this wire.

2. This will help create and maintain all the curves you want.

All the scoubidous in this work are armed.

Crossing scoubidous

1. When you have reached the desired length, place the scoubidou you wish to cross in the centre of the first scoubidou's stitch.

2. Thread the strands on each side of the scoubidou and continue with the usual steps for making scoubidous.

When first pulling tight, check that your strands are arranged properly.

Continue the scoubidou until you reach the size you want.

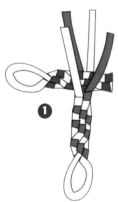

Adding scoubidou strands in a scoubidou

You are making a 4-strand scoubidou and you wish to move on to using 6 or 8 strands.

At the place you want, add a strand in the last loop and pull tight.

At that moment, you can also add 2 strands. You will then start off again with an 8-strand or 6-strand scoubidou, with different colours.

Continue the scoubidou with the preferred stitch. If you have opted for a 6-strand scoubidou with different colours, cut the strand level with the scoubidou after creating 3 full turns.

Finishing off a scoubidou

You will need

Scissors
Craft knife
Soldering iron
Screwdriver

Method

To cut a scoubidou, the stitch has to be even and very tight.

Once you have obtained the size you want, cut off the ends of the scoubidou with scissors.

You can also cut it with a craft knife, especially to remove the knot at one end. In this case, cut it right in the middle of a tightening.

To prevent the scoubidou unravelling, lightly fuse the end with the help of a warm soldering iron or with the preheated tip of a screwdriver.

Do not fuse the end of a scoubidou with a flame – this will blacken it.

It is recommended that children receive some help with this last step.

Using foam sheets

With the help of some tracing paper, reproduce patterns on the foam sheets. To avoid pencil lines, you can do the tracing on the other side (the design will be turned over, once cut out).

Cut the foam with scissors, following the outline of your pattern.

Stick the pieces together or onto the scoubidous. It is preferable to choose glues that do not run. Wipe off any excess glue immediately.

Practical advice

To produce shapes and logos; use armed scoubidous with a round or square simple stitch. The choice is yours, as either will help with the shaping and cutting out. For your scoubidous to become decorative or useful objects, you just need to screw in some eyebolts, so you can then hang them up, or add some rings so you can use them as keyrings. You can also stick magnets to the back of them.

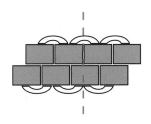

Transport

To produce the following shapes, you must arm your scoubidous. For joins or crossings, let the wire overlap, then stick it in and glue it to the item being joined.

To make a loop in the middle of a scoubidou, arm the scoubidou by following the technique below; at the place where you want the loop to go, sheath the wire with a plastic strand the length of the loop.
Continue the scoubidou.

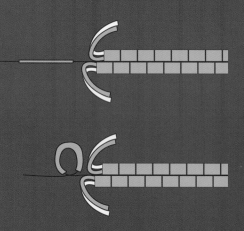

The helicopter

This consists of 5 scoubidous – a 5 cm one, a 2.5 cm one, a 3 cm one and two 0.5 cm scoubidous, a 7 cm piece of sheathed wire, two 4 cm ones (the rear propeller and the base) and a 3 cm one for the cockpit.

The scooter

A 7 cm rectangular scoubidou forms the chassis. The front consists of a 5 cm arched scoubidou and a 2.5 cm vertical one. The back consists of a 4 cm arched one and a 1 cm vertical one. The wheels are made with 3.5 cm scoubidous. A 3 cm scoubidou forms the saddle. The handlebar measures 1 cm. The front and rear lights measure 0.5 cm. The character is made with two scoubidous: one being a shaped 9 cm one and the other a 2 cm one. For the head, stick on a 1 cm polystyrene ball.

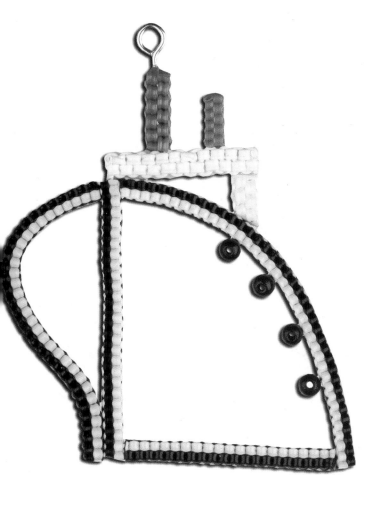

The steamship

The hull consists of 4 scoubidous: a 7 cm (vertical) one, a 5 cm (horizontal) one, an 8 cm (left side) one and a 9 cm (right side) one. Two scoubidous form the bridges – one measuring
3.5 cm and the other 1 cm. There are 2 for the funnels – one measuring 2 cm and the other 1 cm. Four beads are stuck on to represent portholes.

The car

This is made up of three 8 cm rectangular scoubidous for the bodywork and two 2 cm scoubidous for the wheels. A 12 cm piece of sheathed, armed wire is inserted into – and stuck onto – the top scoubidou to form the passenger compartment. Cut a bead in two to make the lights.

Sports logos

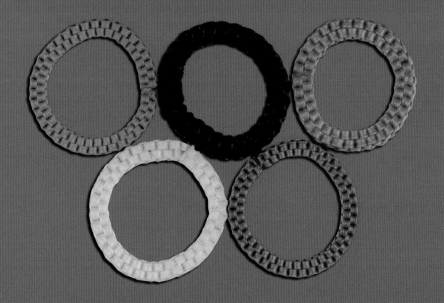

The Olympic Games logo

This is made up of 5 armed scoubidous, each 11 cm long, in the games' colours. Allow 5 mm of wire to overlap. Bend the wire and insert it in the other end, then glue it. Then stick the 5 circles to each other.

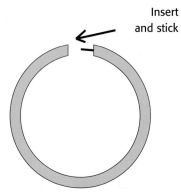

Insert and stick

The weight lifter

Two arched scoubidous form the arms and legs; the first measures 6 cm and the second 7 cm. The body measures 1 cm and the weights 2 cm. Join the 2 weights with a 6 cm piece of armed wire. Assemble and stick on a polystyrene ball for the head.

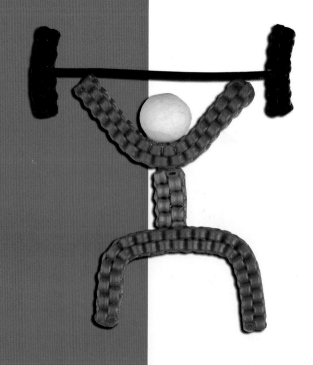

The runner

This is made with 3 scoubidous: a 6 cm one for the body and first leg, a 4 cm one for the second leg and a 2 cm one for the arm.
Stick them all together and add a polystyrene ball for the head.

The gymnast

You will need 4 scoubidous to make this: a 6 cm one for the body and first leg, a 2 cm one for the other, a 3 cm one for the bent arm and a 2 cm one for the extended arm (this has to be cut at an angle).
Assemble and add the head.

The vaulter

The vaulter is made up of 3 scoubidous: a 5 cm arched one for the legs, and two 3 cm ones for the body and arm (slightly curved and cut at an angle, at the shoulder).
The horse is a 1 cm scoubidou into which two 2 cm pieces of sheathed wire have been inserted.

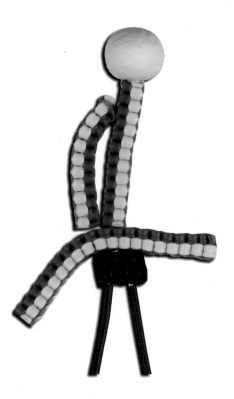

Winter sports

The ski jumper

This is made with 2 scoubidous: a 4.5 cm one for the body and a 2 cm one, cut at an angle, for the arm. The ski is made with a 6 cm piece of sheathed wire. Stick it all together with a polystyrene ball for the head.

The skier

An 8 cm curved scoubidou forms the body and leg. The arm measures 2 cm. Two pieces of sheathed wire symbolise the ski and pole – they measure 7 cm and 6 cm respectively. Slide a 1 cm scoubidou onto the end of the pole.

The ice skater

You will need 3 scoubidous for this: a 5 cm one for the body and the first leg, a 2 cm one for the other leg, and a 1.5 cm one for the arm (which must be cut at an angle). Two 2 cm pieces of sheathed wire, bent up at the front, form the skates. Assemble and add the head.

Water sports

The water skier

The skier is formed with 2 scoubidous: a 4.5 cm one for the body and a 2.5 cm one for the arm. The arm must be extended with a 2.5 cm piece of wire. A 6 cm piece of sheathed wire forms the ski, and another 10 cm one forms the waves. Assemble, stick together and add the head.

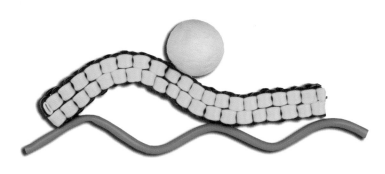

The swimmer

This is made with just one 7 cm scoubidou. Add a 10 cm piece of sheathed wire, shaped like a wave, and the head.

The rower

A 7 cm scoubidou forms the boat, while 2 others form the body and arms – the first measures 3 cm and the second 7 cm. Some sheathed wire represents the oar (10 cm) and the waves (8 cm). Assemble, stick together and add the head, with 2 small pieces of foam to complete the creation.

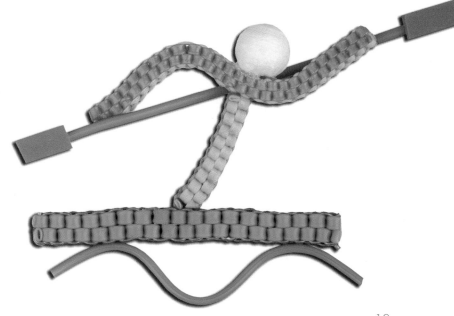

Combat sports

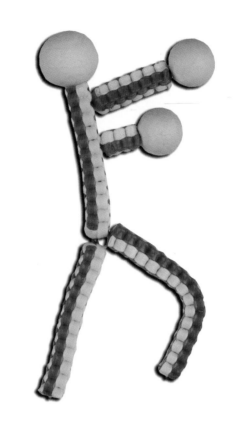

The boxer

This is made with 5 scoubidous: two 3 cm ones for the body and back leg, a 4 cm one for the front leg, and 2 for the arms – one measuring 2 cm and the other 1 cm. Assemble, then stick on a polystyrene ball for the head, 1 cm in diameter, and two 8 mm ones for the gloves.

The judo player

You need 4 scoubidous to make this: a 6 cm one that you curve for the legs, a 3 cm one for the body and two 2 cm ones for the arms. Assemble, stick together and add the head. Make the belt by knotting a strand.

The wrestlers

Two scoubidous form each wrestler. For the legs, you will need two 5 cm scoubidous; for the body and arms, a 4 cm one and another measuring 5 cm (the one on the right). Bend, stick together and add the heads.

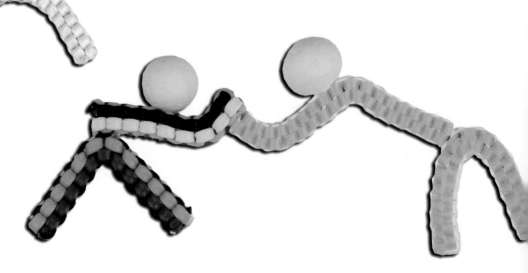

Team sports

The basketball player

This is formed by 3 scoubidous: a 7 cm one for the body and leg, a 4 cm one for the front leg, and a 3 cm one (cut at an angle, at the shoulder) for the arm. Curve, stick together and add the head and ball.

The volleyball player

A 7 cm arched scoubidou forms the legs; the body measures 3 cm and the arm 2 cm. Assemble, stick together and add the head and ball.

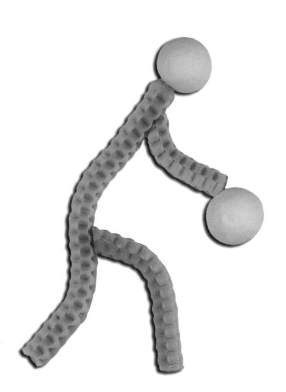

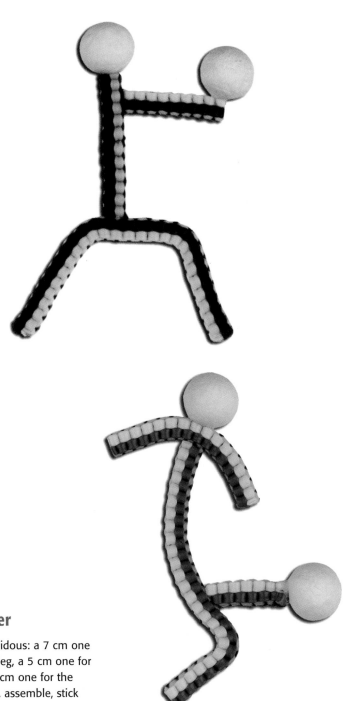

The footballer

You need 3 scoubidous: a 7 cm one for the body and leg, a 5 cm one for the arms and a 2 cm one for the second leg. Curve, assemble, stick together and add the head and ball.

Individual sports

The fencer

This is made with 4 scoubidous: two 3 cm ones for the body and back leg, a 4 cm one for the front leg and a 5 cm one for the arms. Assemble, then glue on a polystyrene ball measuring 1 cm in diameter for the head. At the end of the arm, insert a 5 cm piece of wire, slide on a bead and glue.

The golfer

You will need 3 scoubidous for this: a 6 cm one that you curve for the leg and body, a 3 cm one for the other leg and another, 3 cm long, for the arm. Assemble, stick together and add the head. The club is made with a 5 cm piece of sheathed wire, at the end of which you slide on and stick a bead.

The tennis player

This is formed with 4 scoubidous: a 7 cm one for the body and front leg, a 2 cm one for the back leg, a 3 cm one (cut at an angle, at the shoulder) for the front arm and a 2 cm one for the back arm. Curve, assemble and stick, adding the head. For the racket, sheath an 8 cm piece of wire, leaving 5 mm unsheathed. Insert it into the scoubidou and shape it.

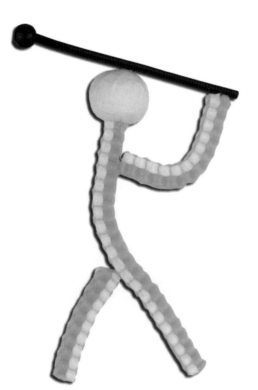

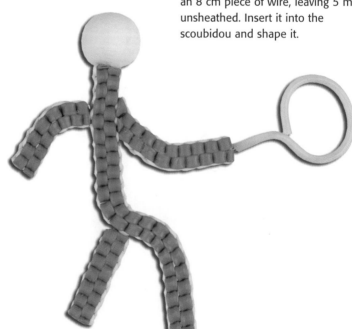

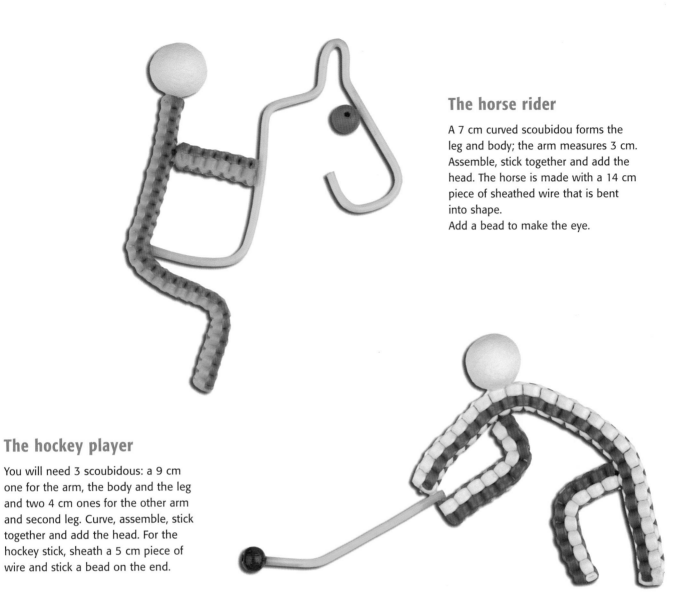

The horse rider

A 7 cm curved scoubidou forms the leg and body; the arm measures 3 cm. Assemble, stick together and add the head. The horse is made with a 14 cm piece of sheathed wire that is bent into shape.

Add a bead to make the eye.

The hockey player

You will need 3 scoubidous: a 9 cm one for the arm, the body and the leg and two 4 cm ones for the other arm and second leg. Curve, assemble, stick together and add the head. For the hockey stick, sheath a 5 cm piece of wire and stick a bead on the end.

The cyclist

A 3 cm scoubidou forms the body, a 2 cm one the arm, a 1.5 cm one the shorts and two 3 cm ones the legs. The wheels are made with 11 cm of sheathed wire. Assemble, stick together and add the head.

Hunting and fishing

The hunter

This is made with 3 scoubidous:
a 6 cm one for the body and back
leg, a 2.5 cm one for the arm, and a
1.5 cm one for the front leg. The gun is
a 6 cm piece of sheathed wire.
Assemble, then stick on a polystyrene
ball measuring 1 cm in diameter for
the head.

The archer

You will need 3 scoubidous for this:
a 6 cm one that you curve for the leg
and body, a 3 cm one for the other leg
and another, 4 cm long, for the
extended front arm and bent rear arm.
Assemble, stick together and add the
head. For the bow, you arch a 7 cm
piece of sheathed wire.

The fisherman

This is formed with 3 scoubidous: a
7 cm one for the body and front leg,
and two 3 cm ones, cut at an angle
where the scoubidous join – one for
the back leg and one for the arm. The
fishing rod is made with a 7 cm piece
of curved, sheathed wire. Shape an
8 cm strand to symbolise the water.

The judo player is
transformed into
a keyring, the
horse rider into a
magnet and the
cyclist into a
straw decoration.

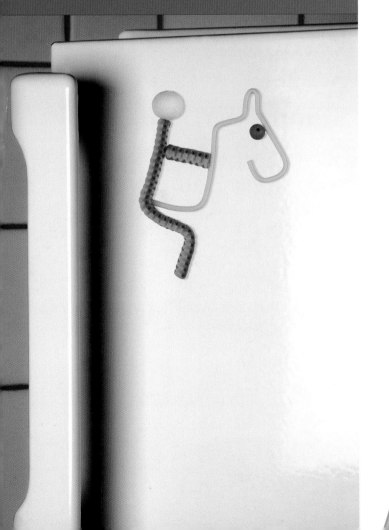

Scoubidous through the seasons

Christmas

Snowflakes

Two 5 cm scoubidous that you can cross (see technique on page 12) or cut and glue together, to which you can stick some small, 1.5 cm scoubidous cut at an angle.

The snowman

The body is made with an 11 cm arched scoubidou, stuck at each end to a 3 cm one. A 10 cm circle forms the head. For the hat, stick together three 1 cm scoubidous, and glue these onto the 2 cm base. Assemble, stick together and add the eyes (2 polystyrene balls with felt-tip dots) and a bead for the nose. The broom is made with some coconut hairs inserted in a wooden bead.

The Christmas tree

The trunk is formed with a 9 cm round-stitch scoubidou. With each turn, and before tightening, add – once in one direction and once in the other direction – an 8 cm piece of wire. When it is finished, cut the wire so that it looks like a fir tree. You can decorate the fir tree with some beads threaded onto the wire, a garland of beads and some small golden objects. Place the fir tree in a small terracotta pot.

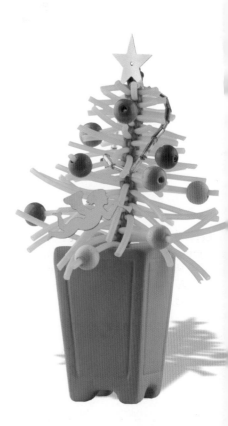

April Fools' Day

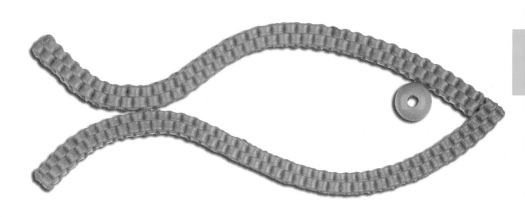

The goldfish

Two 11 cm scoubidous that are bent into shape and stuck together are all you need for this fish.
To complete, stick on a bead where the eye goes.

N.B.: In France, an April fool is referred to as an "April fish".

The clown fish

Make a 26.5 cm bicolour (orange and white) scoubidou.
Cut it into pieces according to the diagram, stick it together and add a wobbly eye – or half a polystyrene ball finished with a felt-tip dot.

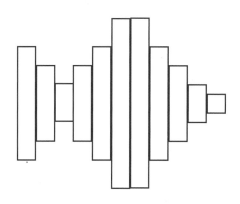

The big fish

Bend and shape your 20 cm scoubidou and secure it with some wire. Finish by sticking on a large wobbly eye – or a polystyrene ball marked with a felt-tip dot.

To make a fish stick to clothes, add a small strip of Velcro to its back.

Easter

The bell

A 15 cm scoubidou with its ends stuck to another, slightly arched, 7 cm one gives you your bell. All you need to do is add a polystyrene ball.

The egg

A 21 cm scoubidou is joined at the ends and shaped like an egg. It contains small 5 cm scoubidous, stitched with several colours and slightly arched.

The chick

A 20 cm scoubidou, whose ends are joined to make a circle, forms the body. Two 3 cm scoubidous are used for feet (bend the ends). Make the beak by following the diagram, using foam or painted cardboard.
Put it all together and stick on 2 beads for the eyes. Glue some feathers on the back of the circle.

The chick's beak

Yellow

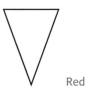
Red

Yellow

Halloween

The pumpkin

A 20 cm scoubidou, whose ends are joined to make a circle, forms the pumpkin. Cut out a circle of foam, of the same diameter, and stick it to the back of the scoubidou. Add the eyes, nose and teeth according to the diagram.

The bat

Two arched scoubidous, each 10 cm long, form the wings. Stick two 6 cm scoubidous on each side. Join it all together with a final, 9 cm scoubidou. Your figure already has style. Add two 1 cm pieces for the ears and stick on 2 polystyrene balls with felt-tip dots. You can stick a wooden toothpick to the base.

The pumpkin

The owl

Three scoubidous are used to form the main part of the head: two 5 cm ones and a 4 cm one. Stick them together to form an "I". In each end, insert a 6 cm piece of sheathed wire (allow a 5 mm overlap for the wire to hold). In the bottom of the scoubidou, insert 4 small scoubidous (see diagram for details). Add 2 beads for the eyes.

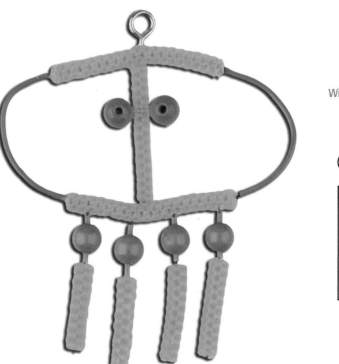

The owl

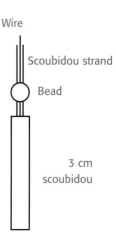

Wire

Scoubidou strand

Bead

3 cm scoubidou

Scoubidou
creations hanging
on a Christmas
tree or on
branches.
The bat is stuck
in the pumpkin.

**Scoubigolos make
fun cocktail sticks.**

31

Scoubigolos

You will find it easy to make these very funny characters using 5 cm scoubidous with hexagonal, turning, rectangular or spiral stitching. Some coloured foam that you cut out according to the diagrams, some polystyrene balls for the eyes, some feathers, some beads and a few accessories such as wooden cocktail sticks, straws, a cork, a magnet, a keyring and some hairgrips will transform the scoubigolos into appealing characters.

The dictator

Hexagonal scoubidou.

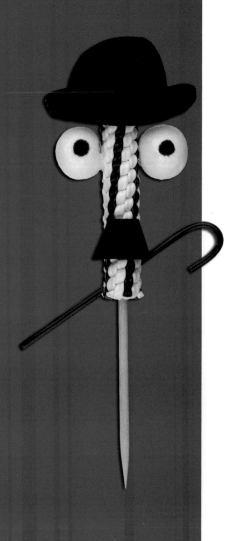

Charlie Chaplin

Scoubidou with 6 turning strands. The cane is made with a 6 cm piece of sheathed wire.

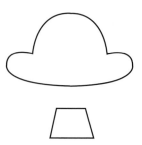

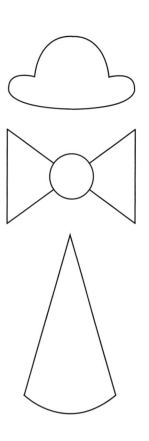

The guitarist clown

Rectangular scoubidou.
To make the guitar, start with a simple, turning scoubidou for 12 turns, add 2 strands and continue for 10 turns, add 2 strands and with another 6 turns, you will finish your double scoubidou.

The white-faced clown

Rectangular scoubidou.
The noses for the clowns and the Oriental man are made with 6 mm beads.

The Oriental man

Rectangular scoubidou.
Draw 2 lines with a felt-tip pen for the eyes.

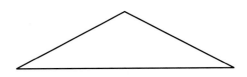

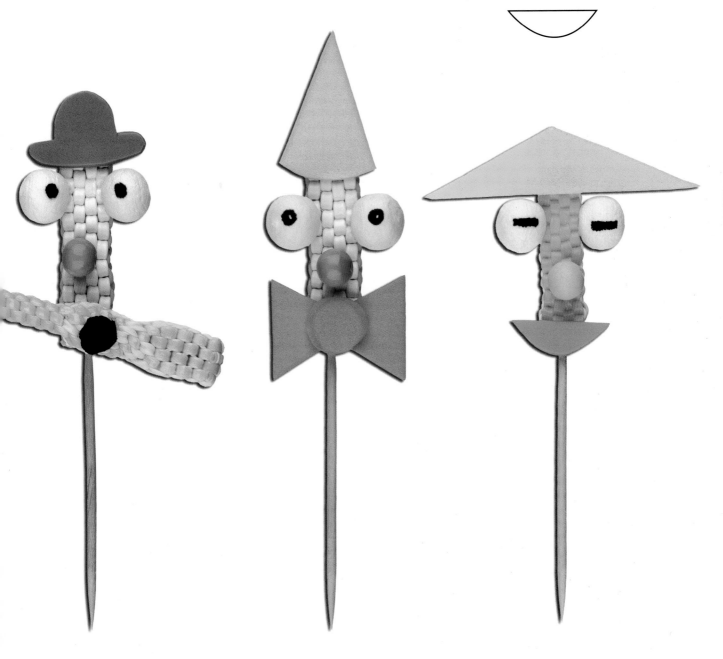

The cowboy

Rectangular scoubidou.
The cut-out foam shapes are stuck down on top of each other.

The blonde

The hair is made with 3 pieces of sheathed wire, measuring 8, 14 and 21 cm. Wrap the pieces of wire round a pencil, curve them and stick them on the top of the scoubidou, starting with the smallest one.

The Native American

Turning rectangular scoubidou.
The arrow is made with a 3.5 cm piece of sheathed wire; the feather is stuck into the end 2 mm of the sheath. The headdress feathers are glued between two 1.5 cm square scoubidous.

The cork with feathers

To decorate the cork, stick together two 3.5 cm scoubidous to make an upside down "V". On the top, stick a pre-painted, cone-shaped cork, a bead for the nose, 2 beads for the eyes and a feather at the back of the cork.

The green mare

You will need: a 6 cm turning rectangular scoubidou for the body, four 3.5 cm turning scoubidous for the legs and a 4 cm simple scoubidou for the neck. Stick a pre-painted, cone-shaped cork on the top of the neck, a bead for the nose, 2 beads for the eyes and a feather at the back of the cork to complete your green mare.

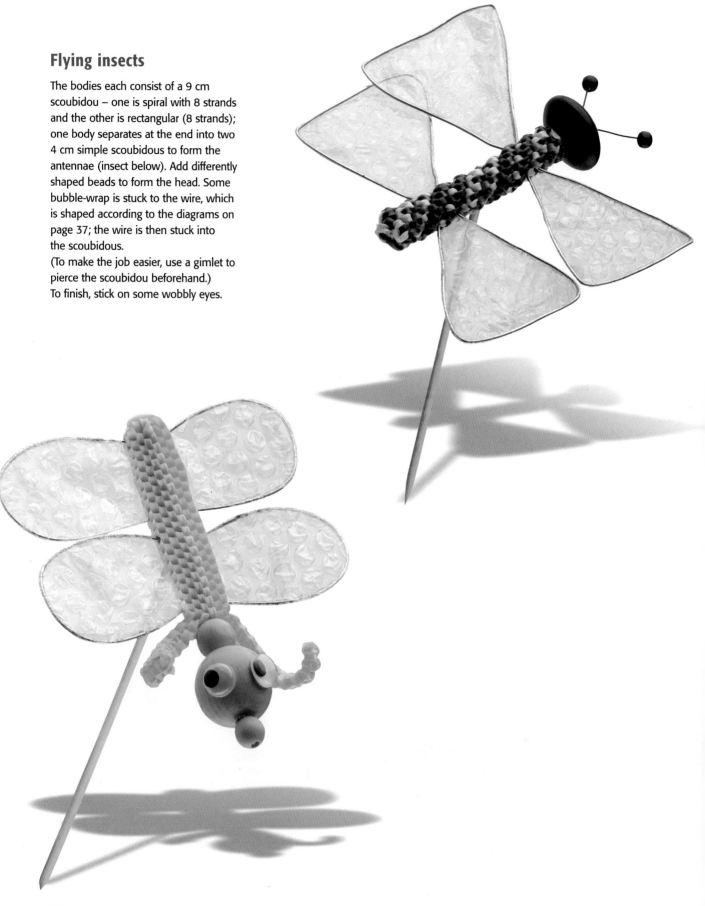

Flying insects

The bodies each consist of a 9 cm
scoubidou – one is spiral with 8 strands
and the other is rectangular (8 strands);
one body separates at the end into two
4 cm simple scoubidous to form the
antennae (insect below). Add differently
shaped beads to form the head. Some
bubble-wrap is stuck to the wire, which
is shaped according to the diagrams on
page 37; the wire is then stuck into
the scoubidous.
(To make the job easier, use a gimlet to
pierce the scoubidou beforehand.)
To finish, stick on some wobbly eyes.

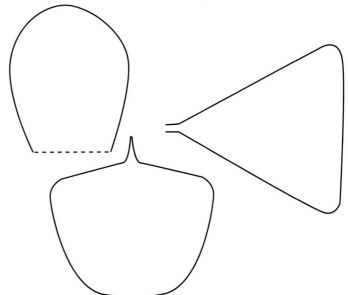

Insect on legs

This consists of 2 scoubidous with different stitching, stuck together. To hide the join, you can use a small piece of foam. The head is made the same way as a simple scoubidou; for 3 turns, add a strand for the antennae and another to enlarge the head, also for 3 turns. A 22 cm piece of sheathed wire, stuck into the ends, spirals round the scoubidou. Stick in the 2 cm legs (sheathed wire) on each side and add the beads. Form the wings with some wire and cut out a piece of bubble-wrap as shown in the diagram. To finish, insert the wings in the body.

Animals on legs

These could be used as knife-rests at a
party. Easy to make, they are open to
all stitching variations.

The wolf

A 6 cm scoubidou forms the body.
Stick on a pre-painted, cone-shaped
cork for the head. Insert some 2 cm
pieces of sheathed wire for the legs
and tail. Finish by sticking on some
beads for the nose and eyes.

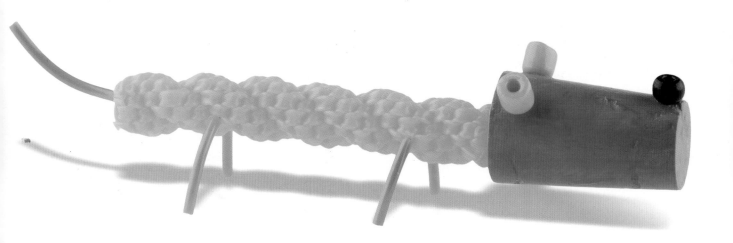

The crocodile

This is made the same way as the wolf.
For the mouth, make a slit in the cork
with the help of a craft knife.

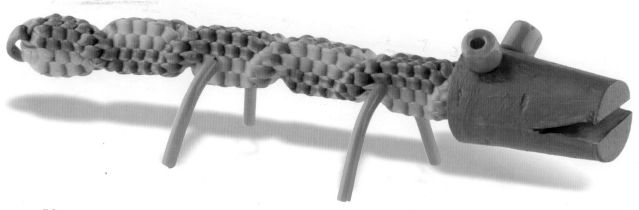

Hanging frames

Make some 18 cm scoubidous in the stitching you prefer. Cut them up as follows: two 5 cm ones and two 4 cm ones. Then stick them onto some cardboard that you have already prepared. Stick a scoubidou strand to the back of the frames, leaving an even space between each frame. At the very top, screw in an eyebolt with a ring.

The photo stand

A 6 cm double scoubidou serves as the stand. The base consists of 2 scoubidous that go round the stand; the first measures 9 cm, the second 13 cm. Insert a 5 cm piece of wire into the top of the scoubidou and stick a peg onto the top of the wire.

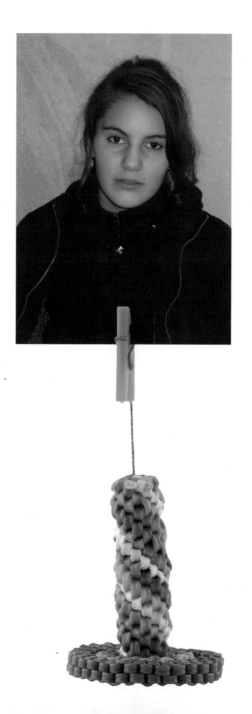

The photo stand
will serve as a
place-card holder
and the crocodile
or wolf will make
an amusing
knife-rest.

The insects can
decorate a plant.

Dream catchers

According to a Native American legend, good dreams go through the web because they know the way, whereas bad dreams are trapped and burn up with the first light of day.

Blue

Make a circle with a 24 cm scoubidou. To hang it up, make a 4 cm armed scoubidou, allowing 4 cm of wire to overlap. Sheath the wire and stick it into the circle. In the same way, make the 2 scoubidous that hold the feathers. To make the web, pierce the circle with a gimlet and thread the scoubidou strand through the hole. Add some beads and feathers.

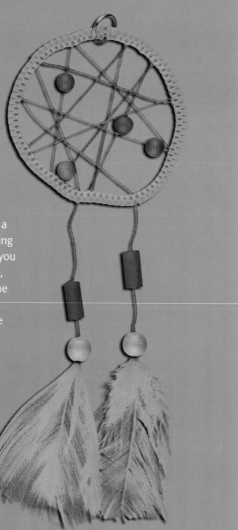

Orange

This technique is the easiest for making the web. Make a circle with a 24 cm scoubidou – but before sticking the ends together, slip on a ring so you can hang it up. Using a large needle, weave some cotton thread across the scoubidou. Add some beads and, at the end of the thread, stick on some feathers.

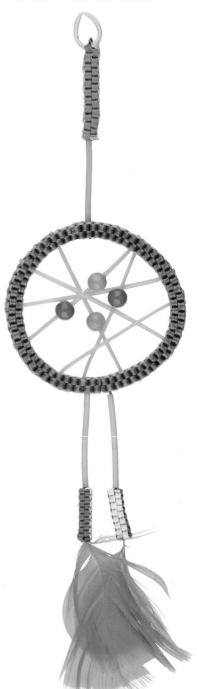

Native American jewellery

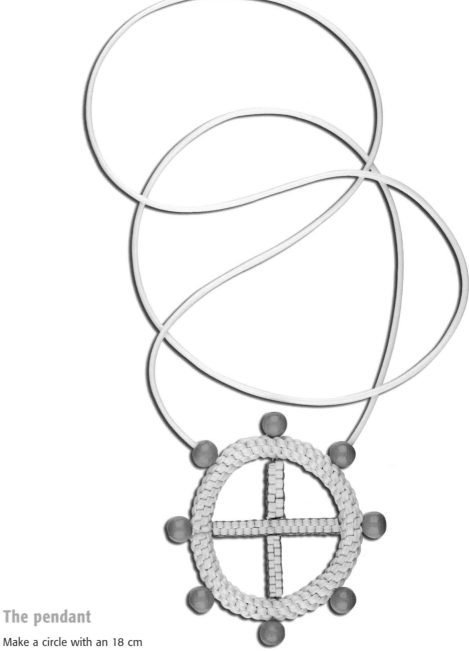

The bracelet

Make a scoubidou that measures 30 cm or longer, depending on the diameter of your wrist, and cut it into 2.5 cm pieces. With the help of a large needle, pierce the ends of the small scoubidous and thread some elastic through, inserting a bead between each pair of scoubidous.

The pendant

Make a circle with an 18 cm scoubidou. Make a scoubidou cross (with the crossing technique or with 3 pieces) and stick it to the centre of the circle. Glue some beads around the outside and add a scoubidou strand to complete the necklace.

Finery

Make some long scoubidous using the
stitching technique of your choice and
cut them up into 2.5 cm pieces. For
the necklace, use the bracelet
technique, described on page 43, on
just one side and make 2 rows. Stick
on 2 scoubidou strands so that it can
go round the neck.
To make the ring and the earrings
(mounts bought in a shop), stick two
1 cm scoubidous side by side.

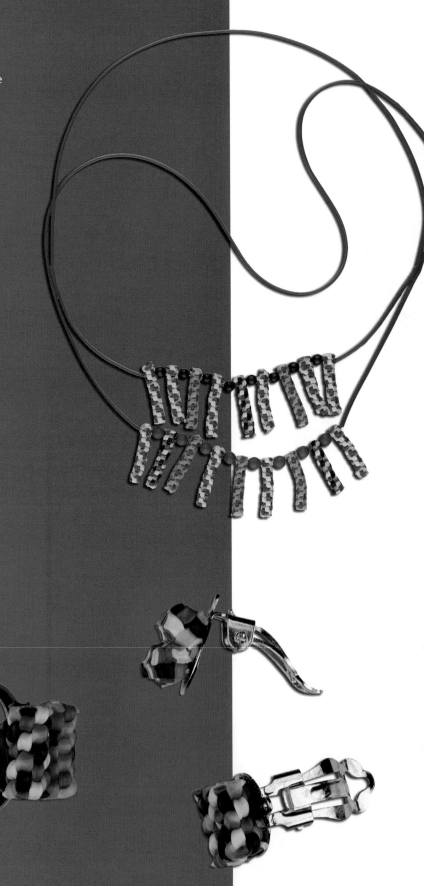

The pendant

Cut out 2 cardboard circles – the first
with a 1.5 cm radius and the second
with a 3 cm radius. Wrap 2 scoubidou
strands round the cardboard circles.
Add a strand to go round your neck.

The matching bracelet

Wrap two scoubidou strands round
some Bristol board that is 3 cm wide
and as long as the diameter of your
closed hand. You will then have a very
trendy bracelet.

Sixties' trend

The sixties' style is back in fashion,
with a look that is easy to create.

Transforming a vase

Take a vase and cover it all over in
double-sided sticky tape. Wrap some
scoubidou strands tightly round,
making sure there are no gaps
between the strands, and alternate
with well-matched colours. To prevent
the ends of the strands unravelling,
add a spot of glue.

A basket

You will find cardboard shapes for making baskets in shops.
Cover both sides of the cardboard with foam that you have already cut to shape. Stick the end of a scoubidou strand to the base, then keep weaving the strand over and under. With each turn, the shape will grow taller. When you change strands, tie or stick the ends and continue. You can change the colour of the strands as you go along. To keep the final turn in place, you can make a scoubidou the length of the basket's circumference – for this model, a 52 cm one – and glue it on.

Scoubidou variations

A nylon cord scoubidou

The stitching technique also lends itself to nylon cord (cord for hanging up the washing); here we have made a band – the snap hook attached to the last stitch can be fastened to the starting-off loop.

The umbrella

Make a 10 cm plait (3 strands), starting with a loop. From this loop, make a round-stitch simple scoubidou for 5 cm, add 1 strand and continue with the round stitch for 2 cm, then add 1 strand. You are going to use the spiral-stitch technique (6 strands) for about 4 cm. Cut the strand that you added last and continue the turning stitch for about 2 cm. Cut the first strand that you added and complete the umbrella with a turning simple stitch for 1 cm.

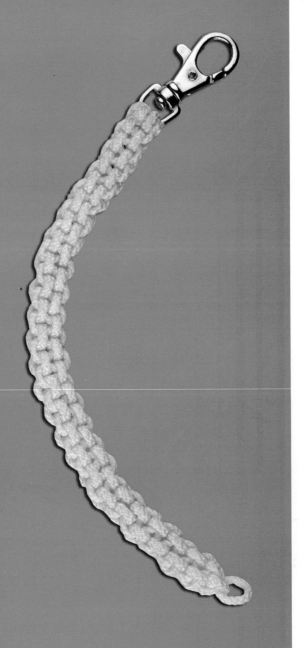